JUPITER	SATURN	URANUS	NEPTUNE
484 million miles/ 778 million km	886 million miles/ 1,427 million km	1,784 million miles/ 2,871 million km	2,795 million miles/ 4,498 million km
11.86 years	29.4 years	84 years	164.79 years
9 hours, 55 min, 18 sec	10 hours, 39 min, 22 sec	17 hours, 14 min, 24 sec	16 hours, 6 min, 36 sec
88,846	74,892	31,764	30,776
Hydrogen, helium	Hydrogen, helium	Helium, hydrogen, methane	Hydrogen, helium, methane
2.14	0.74	0.86	1.10
63	56	27	13
1	1,000+	11	5

SATURN

URANUS

NEPTUNE

OUR SOLAR SYSTEM

S E Y M O U R   S I M O N

Updated Edition

Smithsonian | Collins

An Imprint of HarperCollinsPublishers

For a moment of night we have a glimpse of ourselves and of our world islanded in its stream of stars . . . voyaging between horizons across the eternal seas of space and time.

—Henry Beston

The Outermost House

PHOTO AND ART CREDITS

Pages 4, 8, 10, 23, 25, 27, 28, 30, 31, 36, 40, 42, 47, 58, 60–61: NASA; pages 13, 14, 16, 21, 39, 41, 45, 51, 52, 55: NASA/JPL; page 32: NASA, ESA, and The Hubble Heritage Team (STScI/AURA); page 35: NASA/JPL-Caltech/Cornell; page 47 (inset): NASA/JPL/Space Science Institute; pages 48, 54: NASA/JPL-Caltech; page 57: Dr. R. Albrecht, ESA/ESO Space Telescope European Coordinating Facility/NASA; page 62: courtesy Dennis Milon; page 63: National Optical Astronomy Observatories
Illustrations on the endpapers and pages 6–7, 17, 18, 24 by Ann Neumann

Our Solar System
Copyright © 1992, 2007 by Seymour Simon
Printed in the United States of America.

Library of Congress Cataloging-in-Publication Data
Simon, Seymour.
Our solar system / Seymour Simon.
p. cm.
Summary: Describes the origins and characteristics of the sun, planets, moons, asteroids, meteoroids, and comets.
ISBN-10: 0-06-114008-2 (trade bdg.) — ISBN-13: 978-0-06-114008-2 (trade bdg.)
ISBN-10: 0-06-114009-0 (lib. bdg.) — ISBN-13: 978-0-06-114009-9 (lib. bdg.)
1. Solar system—Juvenile literature. 2. Planets—Juvenile literature. [1. Solar system. 2. Planets.] I. Title.
QB501.3.S63 1992   91-36665
523.2—dc20   CIP
                                                                                                                              AC

13 LP 20 19 18 17 16 15 14 13
❖
Revised Edition

Smithsonian Mission Statement

For more than 160 years, the Smithsonian has remained true to its mission, "the increase and diffusion of knowledge." Today the Smithsonian is not only the world's largest provider of museum experiences supported by authoritative scholarship in science, history, and the arts but also an international leader in scientific research and exploration. The Smithsonian offers the world a picture of America, and America a picture of the world.

In the last fifty years, humanity has learned much about the Solar System, visiting all of the **planets**. The earliest focus was Venus, which had long enchanted humans because it was closest to Earth; a near twin to this planet in terms of size, mass, and **gravity**; and shrouded in a thick layer of clouds.

Likewise, Mars has enjoyed enormous popularity as a place where humans might someday live. Robot explorers have visited it many times and learned much about a Mars teeming with life in its distant past.

Finally, beginning in the 1970s, humans began to send probes to the outer planets, seeking to understand those strange, eerie worlds and their moons. The *Pioneer*, *Voyager*, *Galileo*, and *Cassini* spacecraft have undertaken explorations of Jupiter, Saturn, Neptune, and Uranus. In this effort we have transformed our knowledge of the Solar System and all of its elements.

—Roger D. Launius, National Air and Space Museum, Smithsonian Institution

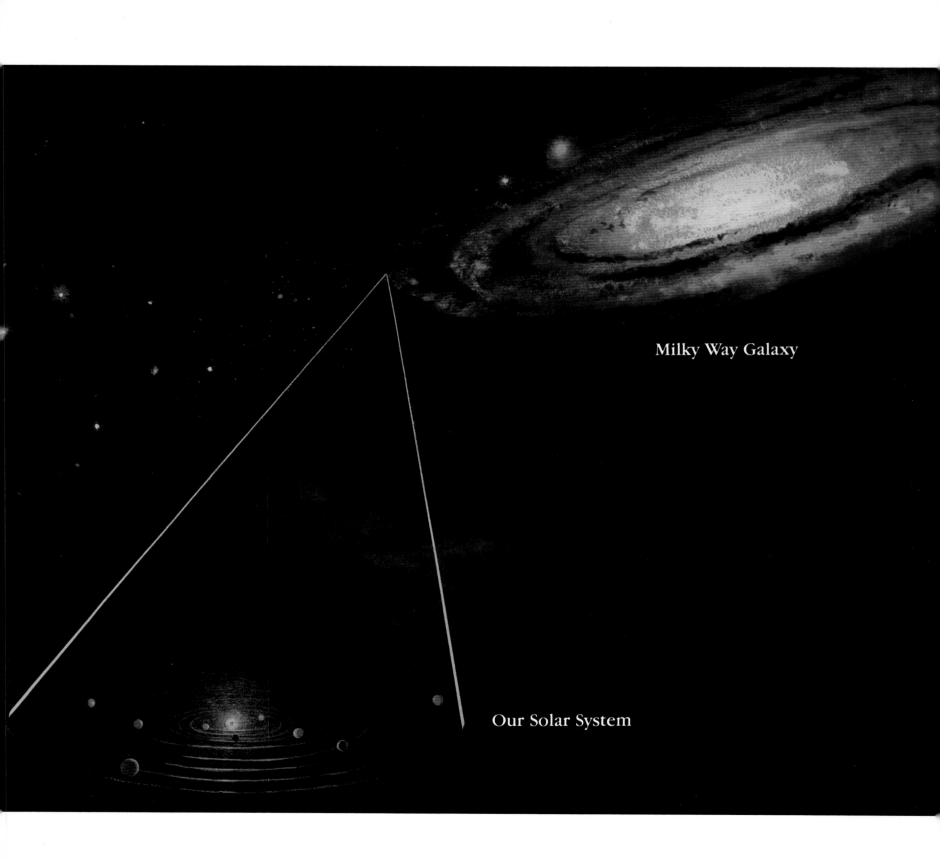

Milky Way Galaxy

Our Solar System

Our Solar System was born among the billions of stars in the **Milky Way** galaxy. About 4.6 billion years ago, a huge cloud of dust and **hydrogen** gas floating at the edges of the galaxy began to pull together to form a globe. The particles packed more and more tightly together and became hotter and hotter. Finally, the enormous heat in the center of the globe set off a chain of **nuclear** explosions, and the sun began to shine.

The blazing sun blasted the nearby gases and dust into a spinning oval ring. As the particles in the ring began to cool, they clumped together into rocky or icy masses called planetesimals. These masses became the rest of the Solar System: planets, moons, asteroids, meteoroids, and comets.

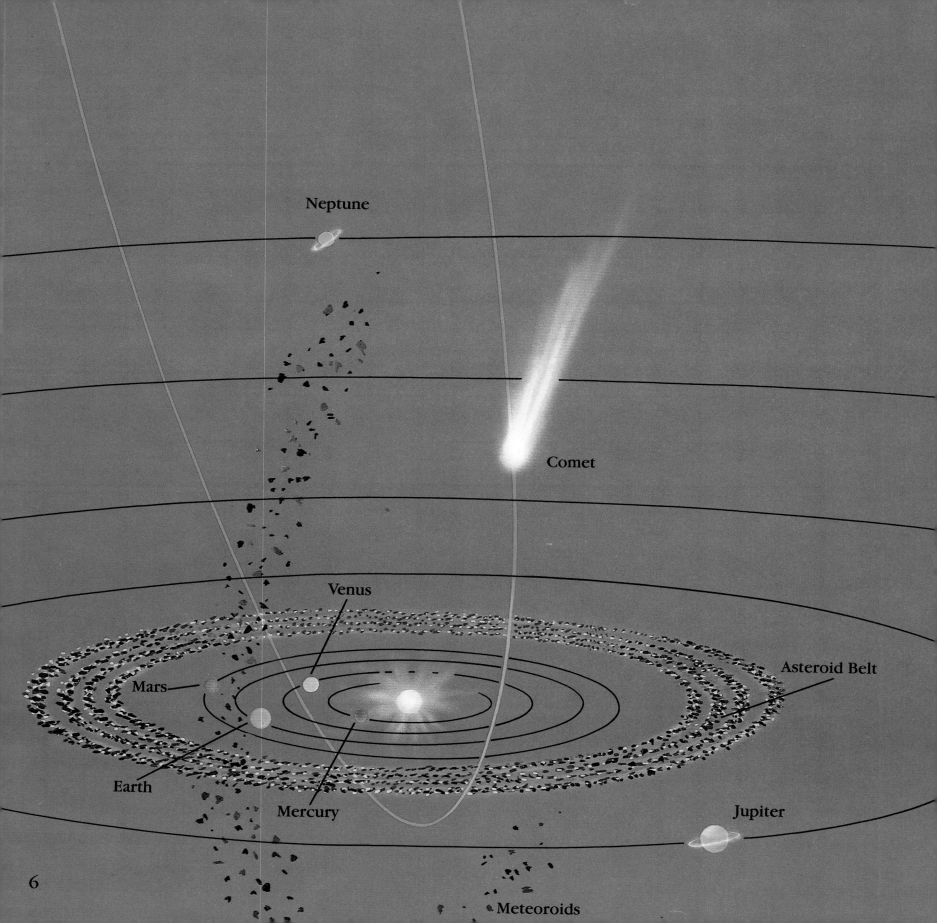

Neptune

Comet

Venus

Asteroid Belt

Mars

Earth

Mercury

Jupiter

Meteoroids

6

The sun is just an ordinary star among the more than 200 billion stars in the Milky Way galaxy. It is not the biggest or the brightest. But the sun is the star nearest to Earth, and the center of our Solar System.

Eight planets travel around the sun in paths called orbits. Mercury, Venus, Earth, and Mars are called the inner planets. These four rocky planets are much smaller than the four giant outer planets—Jupiter, Saturn, Uranus, and Neptune—which are made mostly of gases. Six of the planets, including Earth, have moons circling around them.

Dwarf planets like Pluto and thousands of minor planets, called asteroids, also orbit the sun. Still other, smaller rocks, called meteoroids, as well as many comets, travel around the sun.

Saturn

Uranus

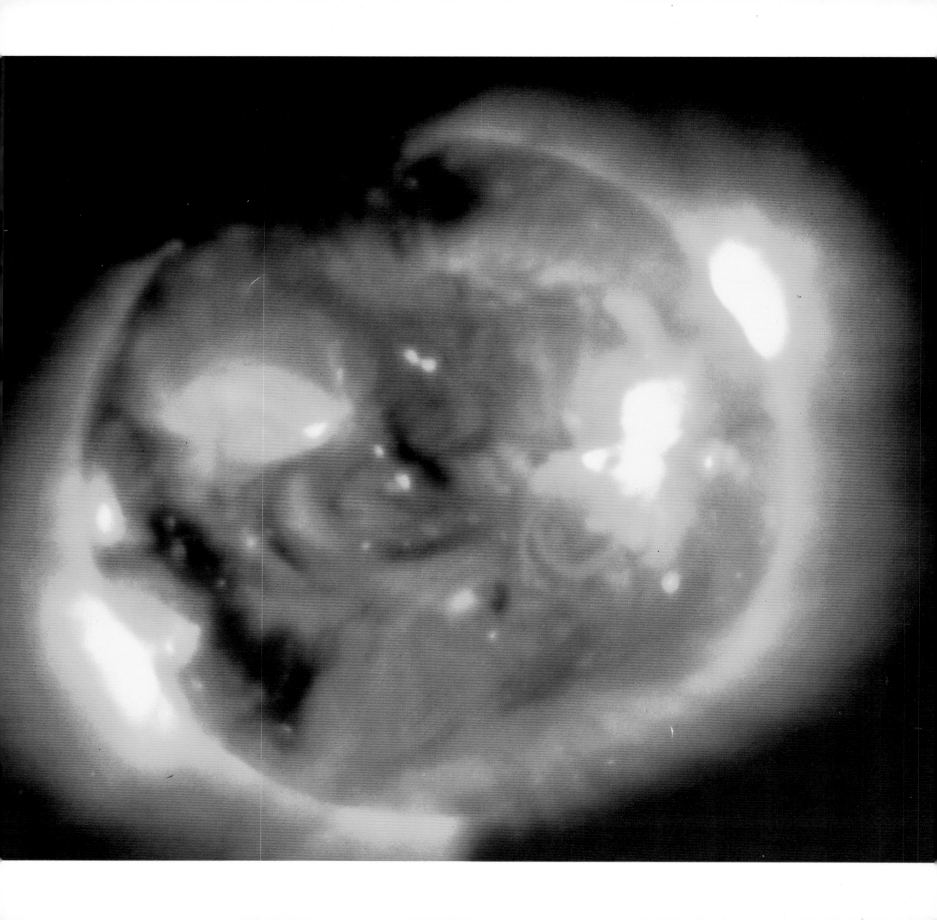

The sun is huge compared to Earth. If the sun were hollow, it could hold 1.3 *million* Earths. If Earth were the size of a basketball, the sun would be as big as a basketball court. In fact, the sun is about six hundred times bigger than all the planets, moons, asteroids, comets, and meteoroids in the Solar System put together.

Hydrogen is the sun's fuel. The sun uses about four million tons of hydrogen every second. Still, the sun has enough hydrogen to continue shining for another five to six billion years.

The sun is all-important to life on Earth. Green plants need sunlight to grow. Animals eat plants for food, and people need animals and plants to live. Our weather and climate depend on the sun. Without the sun, there would be no heat, no light, no clouds, no rain—no living thing on Earth.

The center, or core, of the sun is about as big as the planet Jupiter. Here, constant explosions raise the temperature as high as 27,000,000 degrees **Fahrenheit** (F).

The sun's surface is called the photosphere: a sea of boiling gases about 10,000 degrees F. Giant storms called **sunspots** also erupt on the surface. Flaming streams of gases called prominences sometimes arch up from sunspots through the atmosphere, a protective blanket of air, around the sun. Prominences can travel at speeds of two hundred miles per second and stretch for more than one hundred thousand miles.

The sun has an inner atmosphere, called the chromosphere, and an outer atmosphere, called the corona. The corona stretches outward for millions of miles into space. During a total **solar eclipse**, the corona is visible as a halo around the sun.

Mercury is the closest planet to the sun. It was named by the Romans after their quick-footed messenger god. Mercury revolves quickly around the sun but rotates very slowly on its **axis**, so a day on Mercury is almost as long as two months on Earth.

Mercury is the smallest planet in our Solar System. Mercury is much smaller than Earth. In fact, it is smaller than Jupiter's and Saturn's largest moons. Mercury has no moons.

Mercury is often hard to spot because it is close to the sun's bright glare. It is visible to the naked eye during some early evenings or early mornings when the sun is below the horizon. When Mercury is viewed from Earth through a **telescope**, it appears to change its shape from day to day, similar to our moon.

MARS

MERCURY

MOON
(Earth)

EARTH

IO
(Jupiter)

EUROPA
(Jupiter)

GANYMEDE
(Jupiter)

CALLISTO
(Jupiter)

VENUS

TITAN
(Saturn)

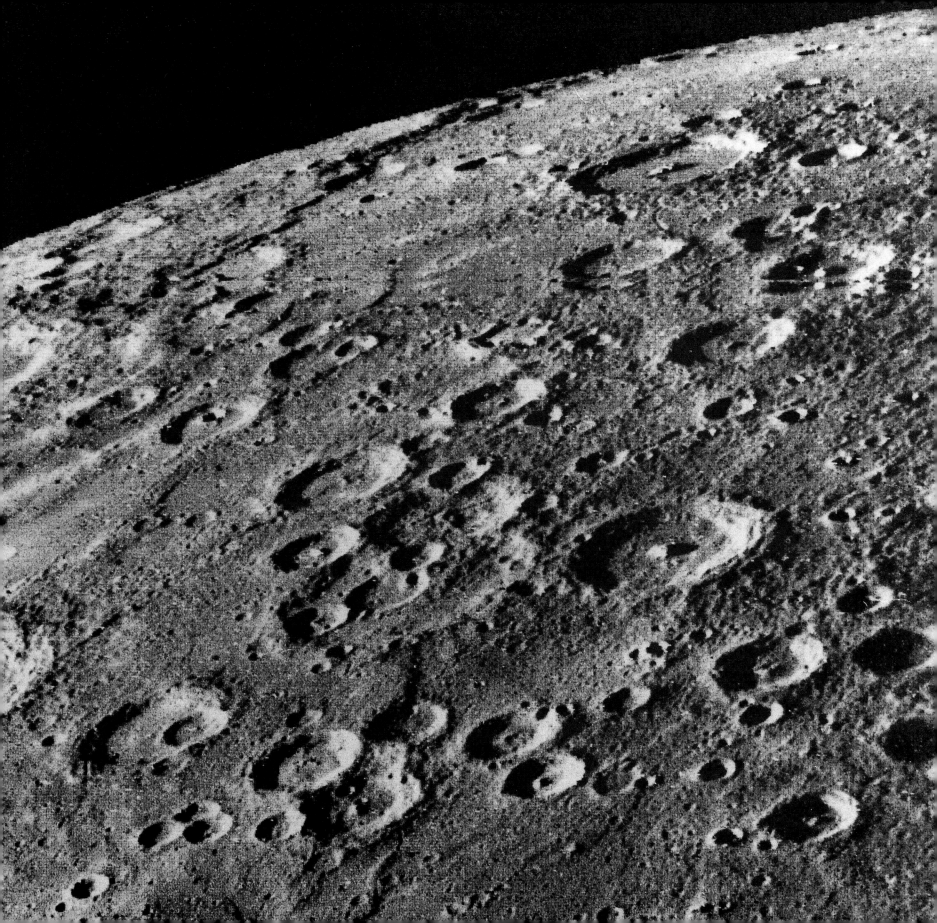

The surface of Mercury has many craters, like on our moon. The larger craters were made by countless meteorites or asteroids crashing into the surface, which is not protected by an atmosphere. Many smaller craters also spot the terrain. Most of these were made when rocks thrown up from the impact of a meteorite came crashing back down.

Mercury is an almost airless planet. The temperature rises above 750 degrees F during the day, hot enough to melt lead. Yet during the long nights, with no atmosphere to trap the heat, the temperature on the dark side drops to -300 degrees F, colder than Earth's South Pole.

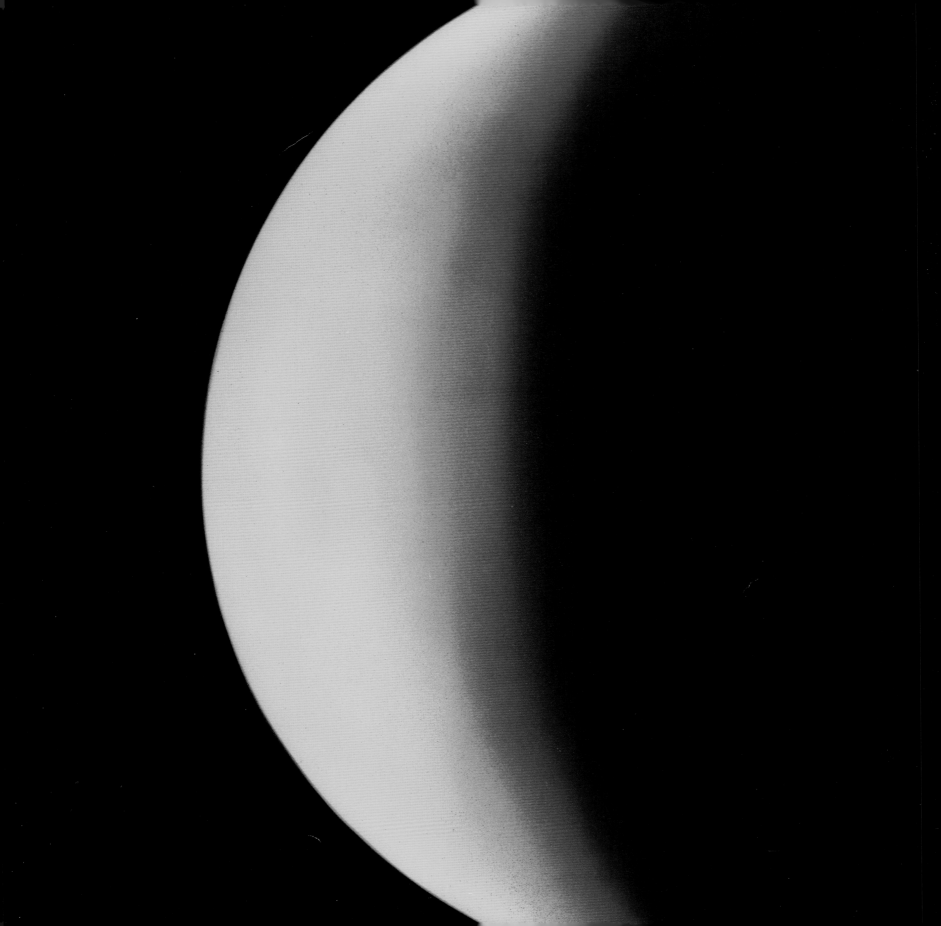

After our moon, Venus is the brightest object in the night sky. The Romans named Venus after their goddess of love and beauty. Venus is sometimes called the Evening Star or the Morning Star. But Venus is not a star. It is the second planet from the sun, between Mercury and Earth. Venus rotates from east to west, the opposite of most other planets and moons in the Solar System. Venus has no moons.

From Earth, Venus seems to change its shape, as do Mercury and our moon. When it is close to Earth, Venus appears much larger than when it is on the other side of the sun. But the clouds covering its surface reflect light so well that Venus appears bright even when it is far away.

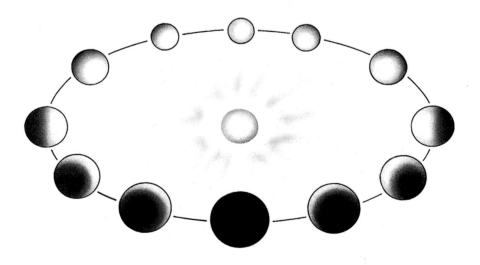

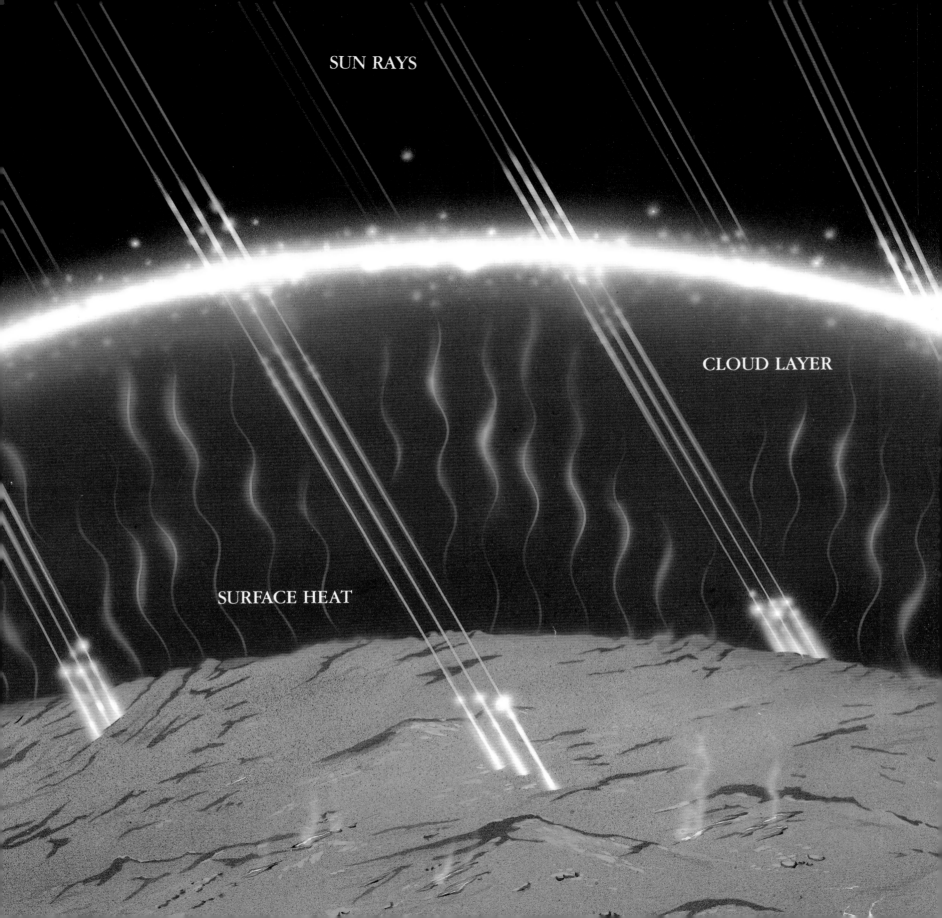

Venus is sometimes called Earth's sister planet because they are about the same size. But Venus is very different from Earth. Like Earth, Venus is covered by thick layers of clouds. But there is very little water on Venus, so the clouds around it are not made of water droplets; instead, they are made of droplets of **sulfuric acid**. Below the clouds is a thick atmosphere of **carbon dioxide**.

Venus is the hottest planet in the Solar System, a desert with temperatures of close to 900 degrees F. Venus's atmosphere is mostly responsible for the intense heat. Sunlight passes through the atmosphere and heats the rocky surface. The rocks radiate heat, and the atmosphere traps the heat so it can't escape. This is called the greenhouse effect because the glass windows in a greenhouse act in the same way.

NASA's *Magellan* spacecraft orbited and photographed Venus for four years. On October 11, 1994, it made a dramatic conclusion to its highly successful mission by crash-landing in order to gain data on the planet's dense atmosphere and on the performance of the spacecraft. *Magellan* has radar-mapped 98 percent of the surface. It uses a special kind of radar that shows details down to the size of a football field, with ten times the clarity of any previous photos.

This global view of the surface of Venus was computer-produced by *Magellan*'s mapping. Venus has large craters but no small ones. That's because the planet's atmosphere is so dense that it stops smaller incoming meteors before they can hit the ground and make a crater.

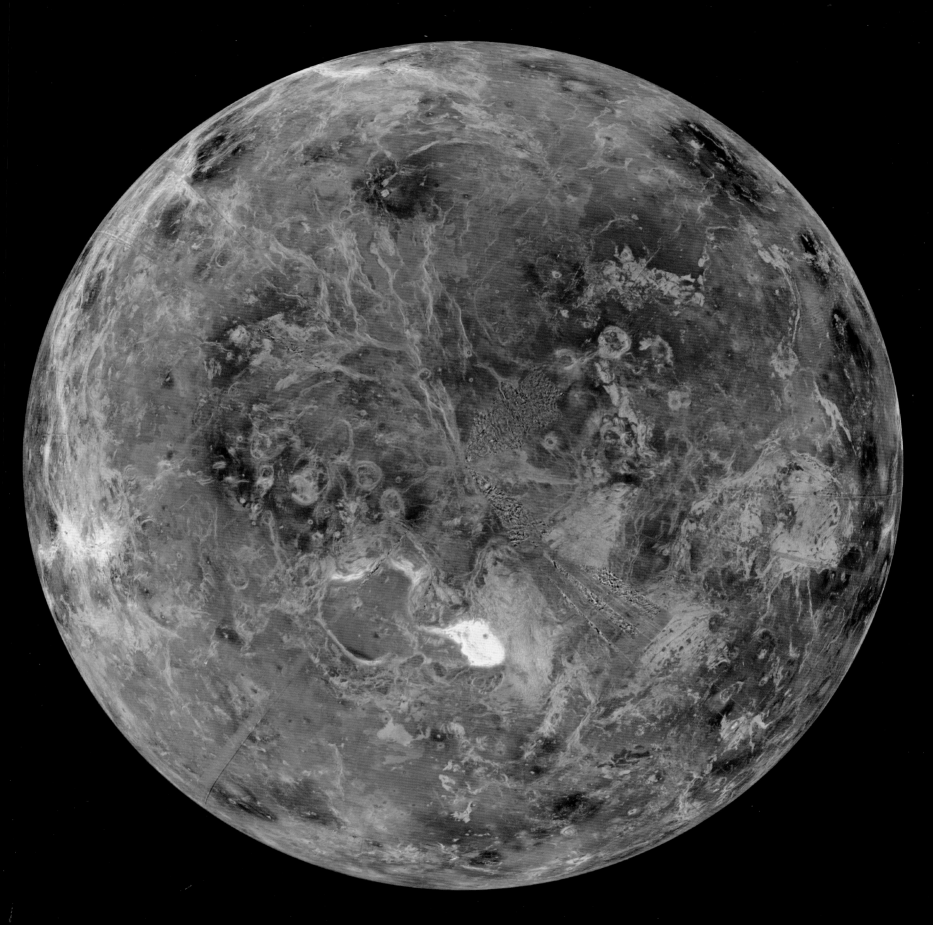

Earth might have been named "Oceans" or "Water." Earth is the only planet in the Solar System with large amounts of liquid water on its surface and in its atmosphere. Earth is the third planet from the sun. If the sun were much closer, the seas on Earth would boil away. If the sun were farther away, the water would freeze over. The sun is just the right distance for life to exist on Earth. As far as we know, Earth is the only planet where there are living things.

This photograph of Earth from space was taken by the Apollo 15 astronauts, the fourth human mission to land on the moon, as they headed home. The brown places are land and the dark blue places are oceans. The white clouds are part of Earth's atmosphere.

Earth is larger than Mercury, Venus, and Mars but much smaller than Jupiter, Saturn, Uranus, and Neptune. From space, Earth looks like a perfect ball. In fact, Earth is about twenty-seven miles wider at the equator than at the poles. As it orbits the sun, Earth spins like a giant top. One complete spin is called a day.

Earth is tilted a little to one side as it travels around the sun. For part of the year, the northern half of Earth has summer because it is tilted toward the sun and gets more direct rays of sunlight for a longer part of the day. During that time, the southern half is tilted away, so it has winter. As Earth continues to orbit, the southern half tilts toward the sun and has summer, while the northern half tilts away and has winter.

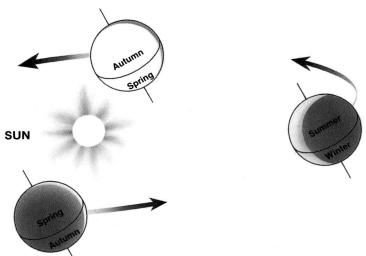

SUN

Earth is surrounded by an atmosphere, which helps keep the temperature fairly steady. The atmosphere is made up mostly of the gases nitrogen and oxygen, along with a small amount of carbon dioxide and tiny particles of dust and water. We live at the bottom of the atmosphere in a five- to ten-mile layer of air called the troposphere. Most weather takes place in the troposphere. The photo shows the spinning clouds of a typhoon in the troposphere over the Pacific Ocean.

Earth is covered by a layer of rocks called the crust, which ranges from 5 to 30 miles deep. The solid crust floats on the mantle, an 1,800-mile-thick layer of heavy, melted rock. The crust is broken into a number of huge pieces called plates. The edges of the plates are called margins. Volcanoes erupt and earthquakes shake the land where these margins crash against each other, such as along the rim of the Pacific Ocean.

Earth's crust is constantly changing. This is a photograph of a mountainous area in the western United States. Mountains are pushed up by pressures within the earth. Cracks in the rocks, called faults, run through the crust. The rocks also wear away. Gravel washes down from the tops of mountains into the valleys below. In the winter, ice breaks up rocks. People also change the land by farming or by shifting the course of rivers to provide water. They dig for rocks and minerals and use them to build roads and cities.

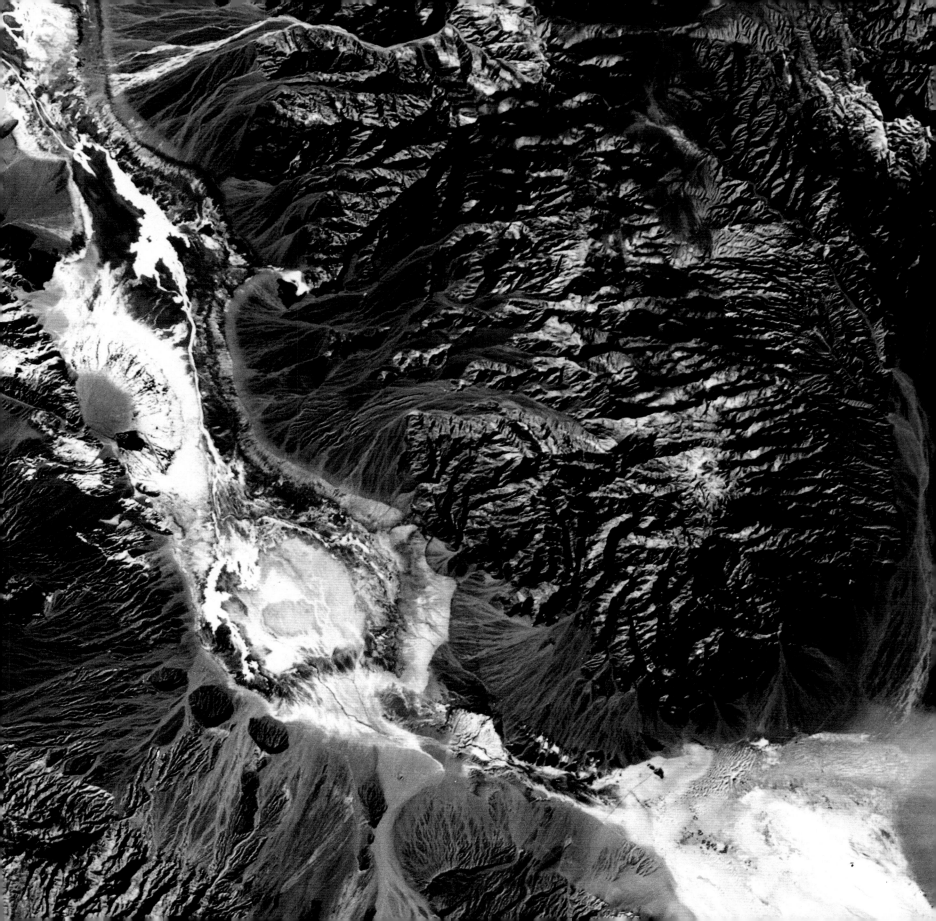

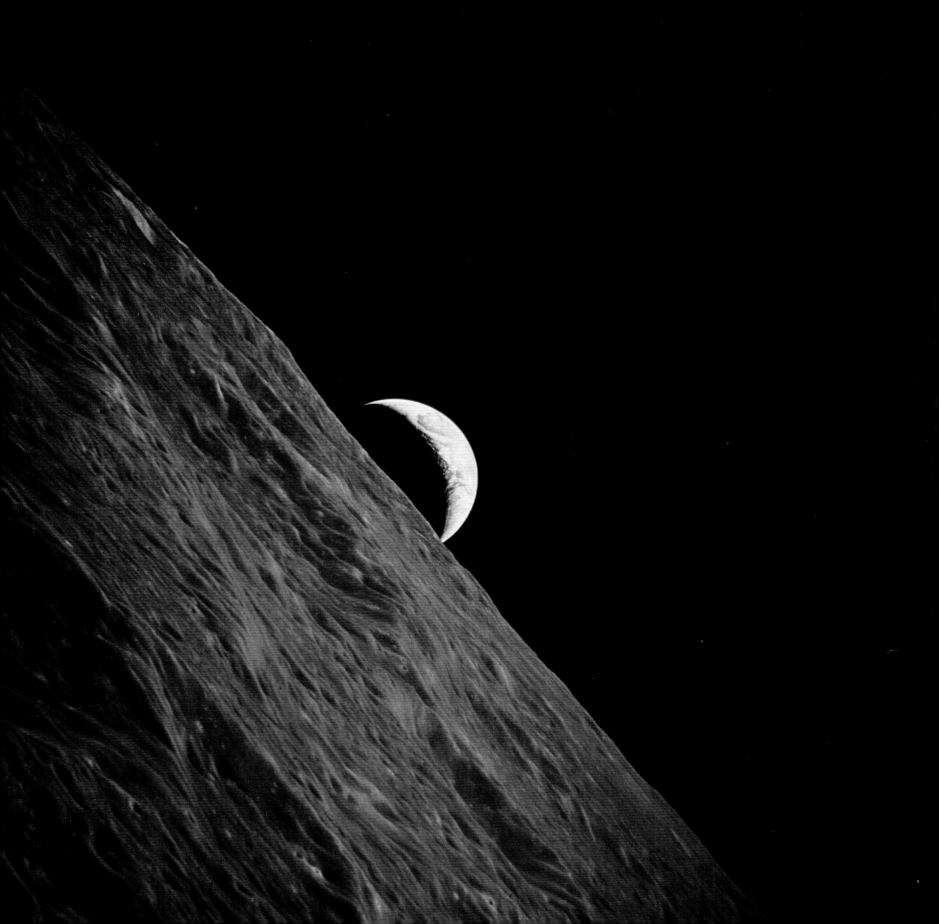

The moon is Earth's closest neighbor in space, only about one-quarter of a million miles away. In space, that is very close. This photo of a crescent Earth over the barren landscape of the moon was taken by the Apollo 17 astronauts in December 1972.

Earth and the moon are close in space, but they are very different. Earth is a blue, watery, cloud-covered planet, filled with living things. The moon is a barren place, with no water, no air, no clouds, and no living things.

The moon is Earth's only natural **satellite**. It is about 2,160 miles across, much smaller than Earth. We can see only the part of the moon lit by sunlight. So every night the moon looks a little different. We call the changes in the moon's appearance phases. The phases go from an all-dark new moon, to a sliver called a crescent moon, to a full moon, and back again to a new moon in about twenty-nine days.

The moon's surface is covered by thousands of bowl-shaped craters. The craters were formed by rocky meteorites or asteroids crashing into the moon, which is not protected by an atmosphere. The fifty-mile-wide crater at the top of the photo is called Copernicus, after the sixteenth-century scholar who was one of the founders of scientific **astronomy**. Some craters are even larger, but most are smaller; some are only a few feet wide. The moon's surface is also covered with mountains and hills, valleys and flatlands.

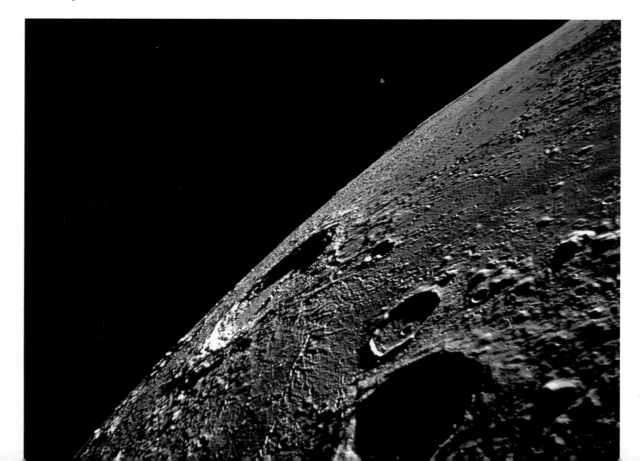

In 1969 and the early 1970s, astronauts from the Apollo space program landed on the moon to gather information. Because the moon's gravity is only one-sixth as strong as Earth's, the astronauts could easily move about on the moon's surface. The moon is about the same age as Earth, but the soil and rocks are different. Scientists think that the moon was much hotter a long time ago and that some of the elements on the surface boiled off into space.

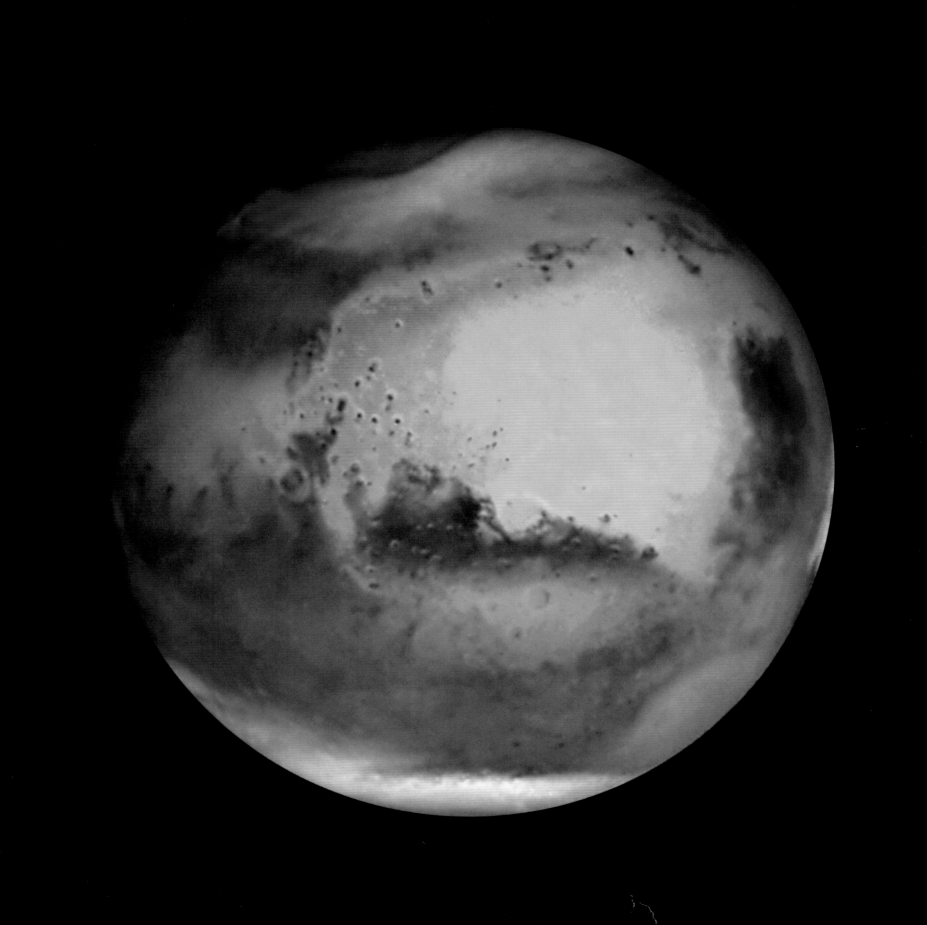

Jupiter is the giant planet of the Solar System, more than one and a half times as big as all the other planets put together. If Jupiter were hollow, more than 1,300 planet Earths could fit inside. Jupiter is the fifth planet from the sun and was named after the ruler of the Roman gods.

Jupiter is a gas planet made up of hydrogen and **helium**, covered by constantly moving clouds hundreds of miles thick. The clouds on Jupiter are mostly hydrogen gas, not water droplets like clouds on Earth.

One of the many mysteries on Jupiter is a giant windstorm called the Great Red Spot. The spot is nearly three times the size of Earth. It was first seen through a telescope more than three hundred years ago. At different times, it has shrunk or grown, turned dull pink or bright red. But it has not changed position and has kept the same oval shape for centuries.

One of the *Voyager* spacecraft's most exciting discoveries was that Jupiter has rings circling the planet. The photograph (right) was taken by the *Galileo* spacecraft in 1996 and shows Jupiter's rings. All the four giant outer planets—Jupiter, Saturn, Uranus, and Neptune—which are composed mostly of gases, have rings.

Jupiter is unlike Earth in many ways. The temperature at the cloud tops is very cold—more than 250 degrees F below freezing. Its surface is an ocean of liquid hydrogen that may be ten thousand or more miles deep. At its center, Jupiter is very hot. The heat from below stirs up the liquid hydrogen and the cloud tops, so that they rise and sink. Life as we know it could not exist on Jupiter. Jupiter and the outer planets are strange and unfamiliar places that we have only begun to explore.

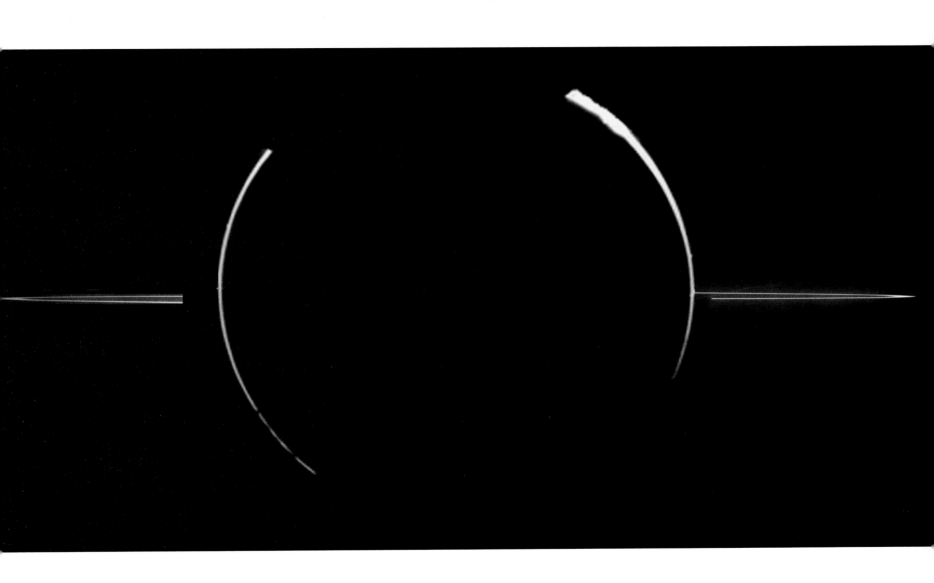

Jupiter has more known moons than any other planet in the solar system. Jupiter has sixteen major moons and at least forty-seven minor ones. The four largest moons are named Io, Europa, Ganymede, and Callisto. These are called the Galilean moons, after Galileo, the great scientist who discovered them in 1610 with his small homemade telescope. The minor moons are small. Most are less than fifty miles across and have odd shapes. Many of these are thought to be asteroids that were captured by Jupiter's strong gravity.

Spaceships such as *Galileo* have given us close-up looks at the moons of Jupiter. Ganymede is the biggest moon in the Solar System, larger than the planet Mercury. Callisto is icy, with small amounts of rock on top of a deep, frozen ocean.

Europa (both images below) is about the size of Earth's moon. It has a frozen icy crust and may have a cold, saltwater ocean beneath. If there is liquid water beneath the crust, then Europa may be one of the likeliest places in the Solar System for microscopic life.

Io has something that no other moon in the Solar System has: exploding volcanoes. The volcanoes often erupt, sending out flows of hot liquid sulfur. The surface of Io changes with each new eruption because the sulfur changes color as it cools.

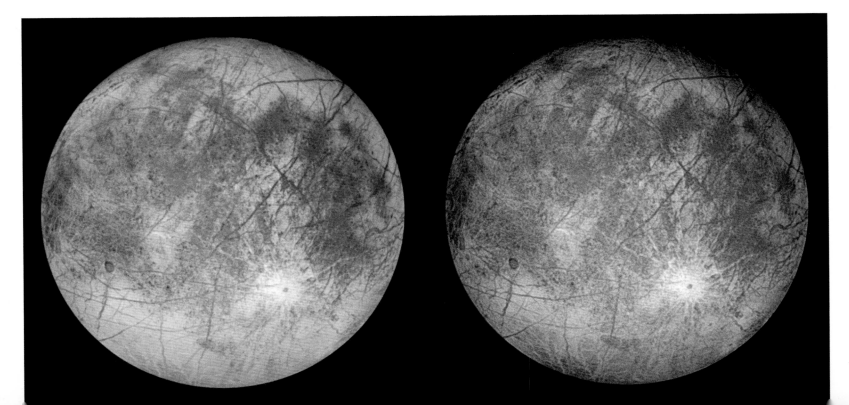

Saturn is the second-largest planet, after Jupiter. If Saturn were hollow, about 750 planet Earths could fit inside. Like Jupiter, Saturn is a gas planet, made up mostly of hydrogen and helium. Saturn is the sixth planet from the sun and was named after the Roman god of farming.

Galileo looked at Saturn through his low-power telescope nearly four centuries ago. He was shocked to see what looked like ears on either side of the planet. Galileo decided that they were two smaller globes. About fifty years later, an astronomer with a stronger telescope saw that the two globes were really a flat ring around the planet.

Even if you look through a powerful telescope on Earth, Saturn appears to have just a few rings. But spacecraft photos, like this one by the *Cassini* orbiter, show that the large rings are made of thousands of smaller rings. If you were to get closer, you would see that the rings are made of pieces of ice. Some are as small as a fingernail; others, as big as a house. The rings also contain dust and bits of rock. And all the materials in the rings spin around Saturn like millions of tiny moons.

The rings are nearly 17,000 miles across but are less than 3 miles thick, and some are even thinner. How did the rings form? Some scientists think that the rings around the gas planets contain materials left over when the planets formed. Perhaps pieces of nearby moons that were chipped off by incoming meteorites helped to form rings. No one knows for sure.

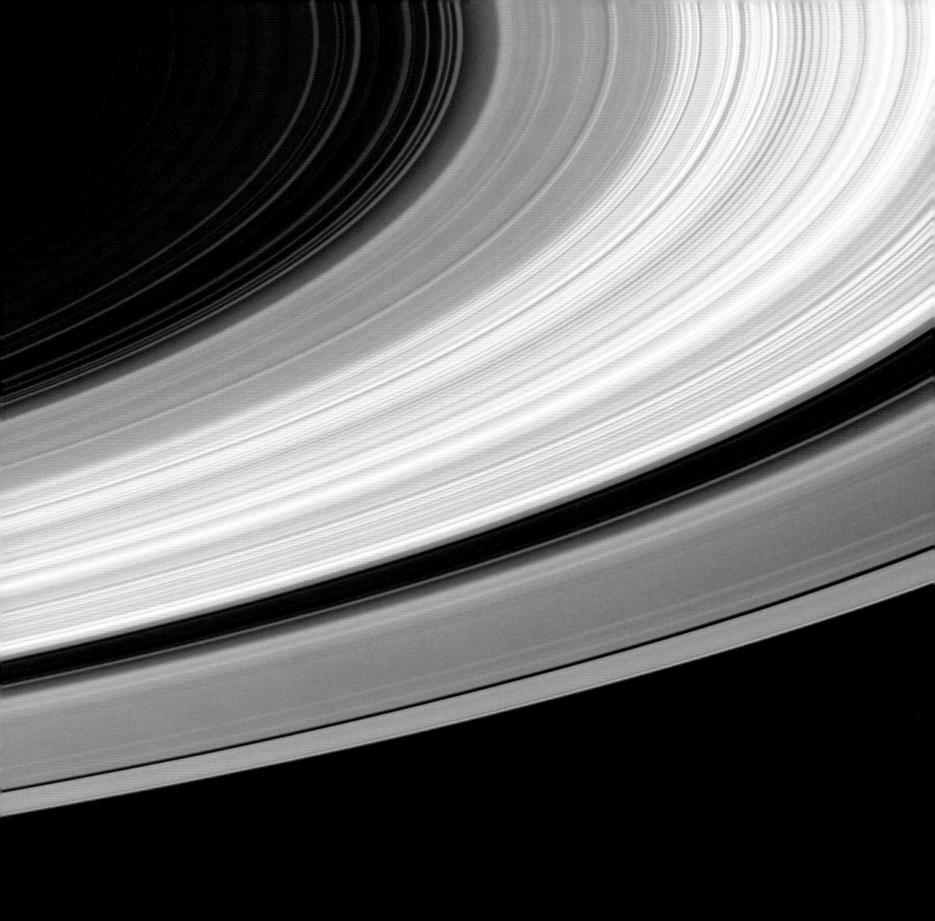

Saturn has one large moon and six medium-sized moons among its fifty-six satellites. Most of Saturn's moons are ice-covered and marked with craters.

This picture of Saturn and some of its moons was made from a number of photographs taken by *Voyager*. Saturn is partly hidden by the moon Dione. Enceladus and Rhea are off in the distance to the upper left. Tethys and Mimas are off to the lower right. Titan, Saturn's largest moon, is far away at the top right and in the inset photo. Titan is bigger than the planet Mercury. In 2006, the *Cassini* spacecraft discovered that Enceladus is shooting out a giant plume of water vapor. The discovery has led scientists to believe this moon of Saturn might have a liquid ocean under its icy surface.

Titan is the only moon in the Solar System known to have an atmosphere. On January 14, 2005, the European Space Agency's Huygens probe reached the upper layer of Titan's atmosphere and landed on the surface after a parachute descent of two hours and twenty-eight minutes. The probe found that Titan's atmosphere is mostly nitrogen gas and covers the surface with a thick haze.

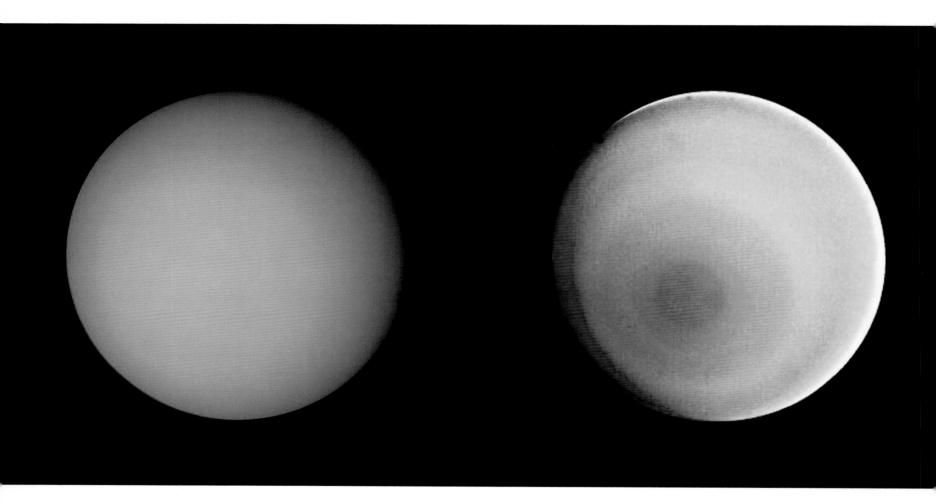

Uranus is the seventh planet from the sun. Years after its discovery by William Herschel through a telescope in 1781, the planet was named Uranus, after the Greek god of heaven and ruler of the world. Uranus is a ringed planet made up mostly of gases, about halfway in size between Jupiter and Earth. If Uranus were hollow, about fifty planet Earths could fit inside.

In January 1986, eight and a half years after it had been launched from Earth, the *Voyager 2* spacecraft swept past the pale blue-green clouds of Uranus. These two photographs of Uranus—in true color (left) and false color (right)—were taken by *Voyager 2*.

Uranus is tipped on its side in space. At this time, the south end of the axis is pointing at the sun. Therefore, the south pole is having forty-two years of constant sunlight, while the north pole is having forty-two years of night. Gradually the north pole will point at the sun, and it will have forty-two years of sunlight, while the south pole will be dark.

Uranus has five large moons and at least twenty-two smaller ones. Many of the smaller moons are icy and have strange surface features. This view shows part of Miranda, innermost of the five larger moons, circling only sixty-five thousand miles away from the cloud tops of Uranus. Miranda is the most unusual of the moons. Huge canyons, deep grooves, ridges, and ropelike markings cover its surface—all this on a moon only three hundred miles across.

Uranus has eleven thin rings, along with pieces or arcs of other rings. The rings are made of chunks of an unknown black material that spins around Uranus like lumps of coal on a merry-go-round.

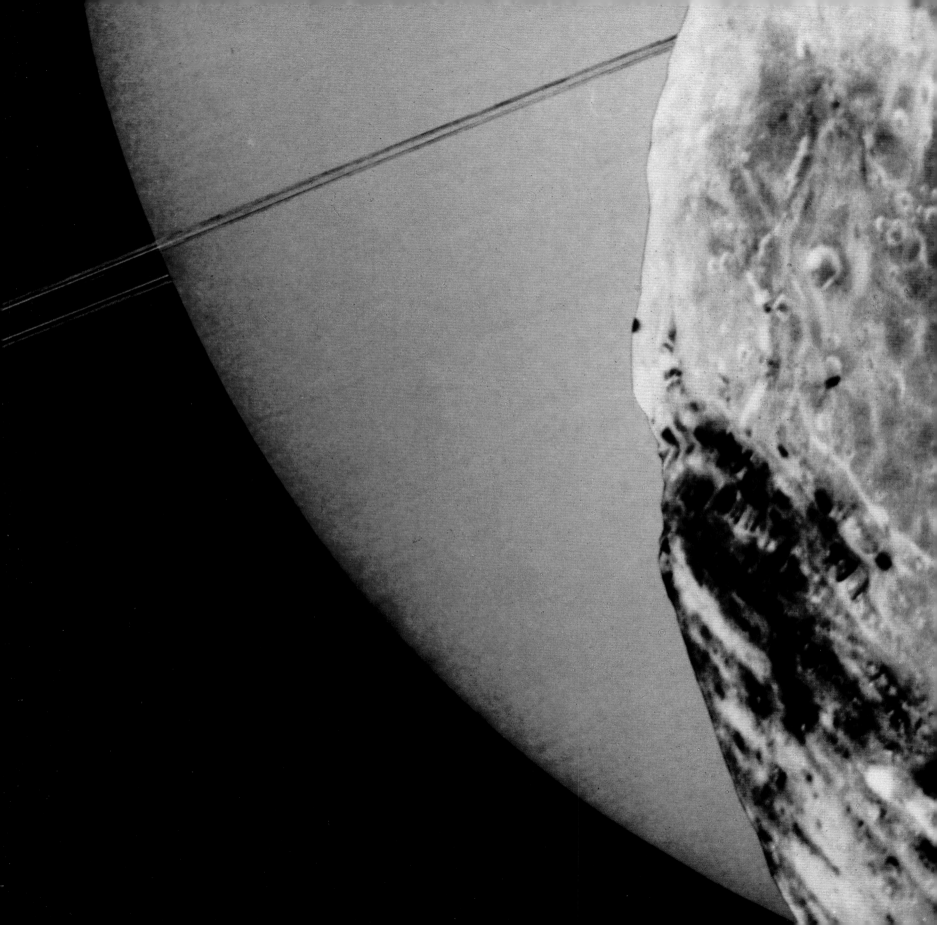

Neptune is too far from Earth to be seen without a telescope. Galileo saw Neptune through his small telescope but mistook it for a star. It was first identified as a planet in 1846. Later it was named Neptune, after the Roman god of the sea. Neptune is just a bit smaller than Uranus.

Neptune is a ringed gas planet with dark storms, giant hurricanes, and streaky white clouds of **methane** ice that float thirty-five miles above the lower cloud deck. The largest storm is big enough to swallow the entire earth. Strong, frigid winds in the atmosphere blow at the fastest speeds ever measured on a planet, up to seven hundred miles per hour. Methane in the atmosphere absorbs the red light from the sun but reflects the blue light back into space. This is why Neptune appears blue. Haze high above the clouds causes the red rim.

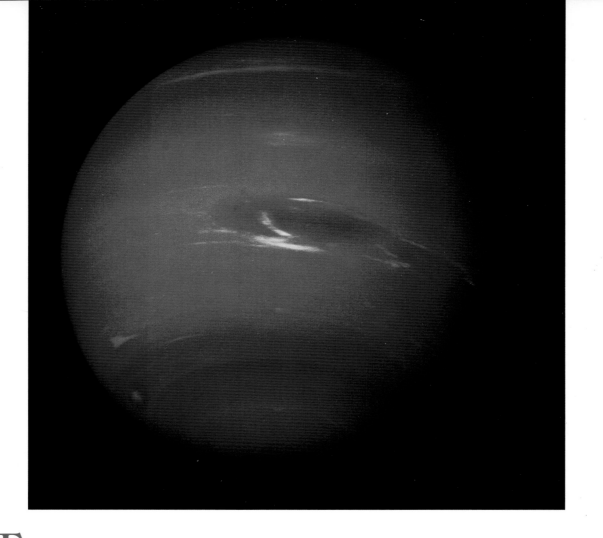

Twelve years and more than 2.8 billion miles after leaving Earth, *Voyager 2* whizzed past Neptune on August 25, 1989, and headed on its way out of the Solar System. The spacecraft found that Neptune has two bright outer rings, a fainter inner ring, and a thin ring of dusty material. Scientists still need more time to examine and understand all the information *Voyager 2* has provided about the outer planets.

"A world unlike any other" is how scientists described Neptune's moon Triton. Neptune has at least thirteen moons, two large ones and eleven smaller ones. Triton is the biggest, about 1,700 miles across, nearly the same size as our own moon. Triton is colder than any other object ever measured in the Solar System. Large parts of the satellite look like the rind of an orange, with gigantic cracks running across the surface. Triton has geysers that shoot ice five miles high into its thick atmosphere. There may be water under the ice on Triton. It's even possible that there may be microscopic life in the water.

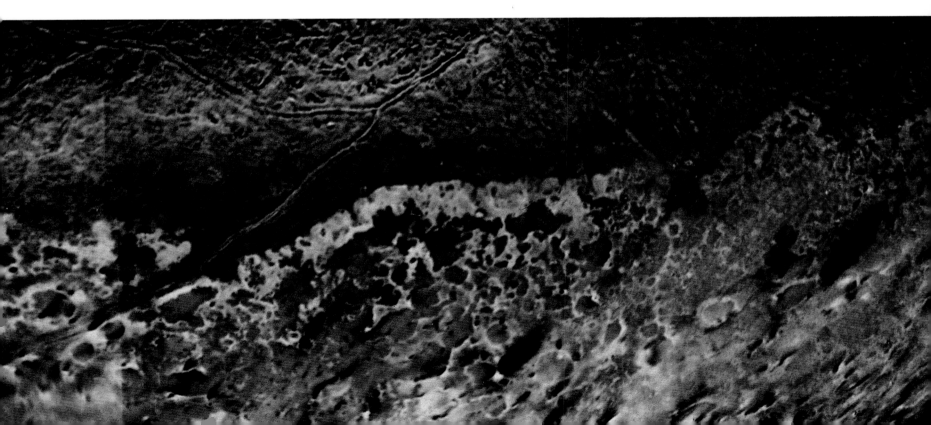

Discovered in 1930, Pluto had remained undetected for many years because it is so far from Earth and less than two-thirds the size of Earth's moon. Pluto was named after the Greek and Roman god of the underworld. It was long thought to be the smallest, coldest planet of our solar system.

In 1978, astronomers discovered that tiny Pluto has a large moon of its own and named it Charon, after the boatman on the river Styx in the underworld. Charon's diameter is slightly over half of Pluto's. Charon revolves close to Pluto and speeds through its orbit in only six days and nine hours. This is a photo (facing page) of Pluto (left) and Charon (right).

Scientists now use three ways to classify a planet: 1. It must orbit the sun. 2. It must be big enough for gravity to squeeze the planet into the shape of a basketball. 3. The planet must clear other smaller rocky or icy bodies out of its way when it orbits around the sun.

In 2006, scientists decided that Pluto should not be called a planet at all since it cannot clear bodies as it's orbiting the sun. This third rule of planet classification is what demoted Pluto from planet status to a dwarf planet. A dwarf planet only has to be round and orbit the sun. Pluto is one of the largest of a group of icy balls

of frozen rock and gases that exist far beyond the orbit of Neptune in a region called the Kuiper Belt.

In the new definition of the Solar System, there are eight planets, at least three minor, or dwarf, planets, and tens of thousands of much smaller Solar System objects, such as comets and asteroids.

For now, the dwarf, or smaller, planets include Pluto; Ceres, the largest asteroid; and Eris. Discovered in 2003, Eris is larger than Pluto and orbits in the Kuiper Belt far beyond Neptune. But there are dozens more dwarf planets in the Kuiper Belt, scientists say. Who knows what other new discoveries scientists will make about the Solar System?

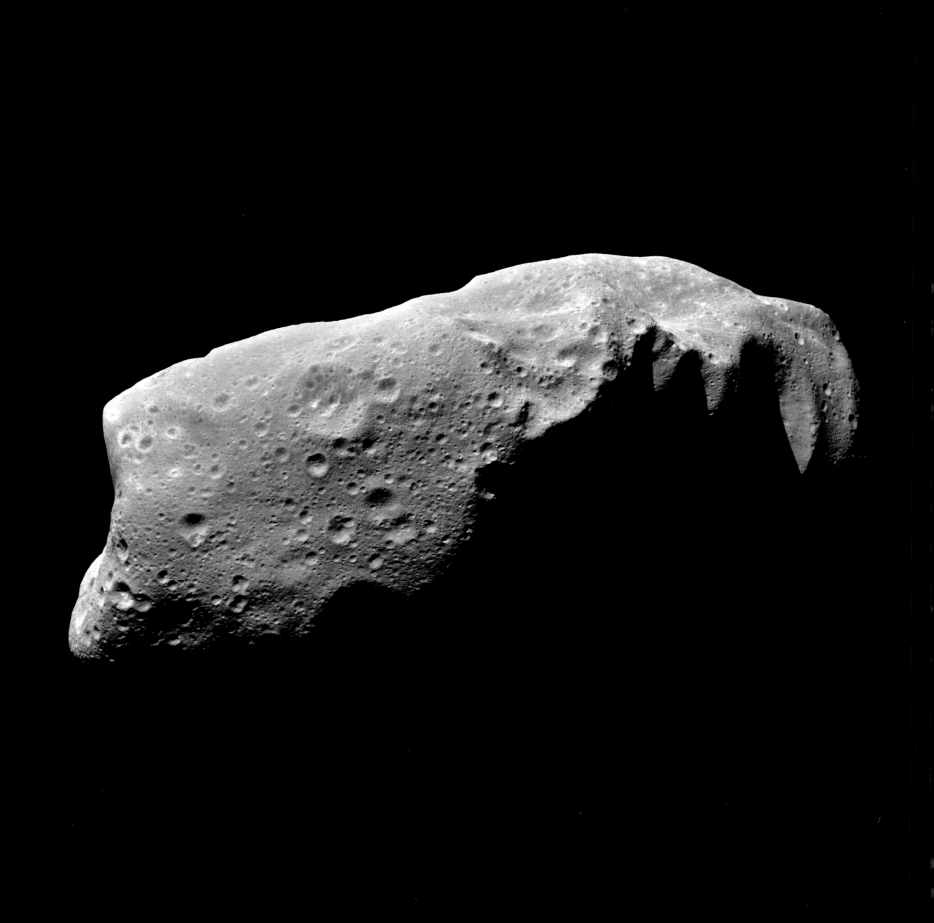

Asteroids are very small worlds that circle the sun, mainly between the orbits of Mars and Jupiter, a region called the asteroid belt. About three thousand asteroids have been discovered, but scientists think that there are many thousands more.

Sometimes called minor planets, all the asteroids combined would not make a world as large as our moon. Most are only a few miles across. Ceres, about six hundred miles in diameter, is by far the largest asteroid. Pallas and Vesta are the next largest asteroids, both more than three hundred miles in diameter.

Apollo asteroids are a small group that swings in close to the sun and may approach Earth. In 1937, a small asteroid, Hermes, came within a million miles of Earth. That's a close brush in space. Will an asteroid ever hit Earth, and what would happen if it did? Some scientists think that asteroids (or comets) have hit our planet in the past and may hit it in the future. They say that one such impact resulted in the extinction of the dinosaurs.

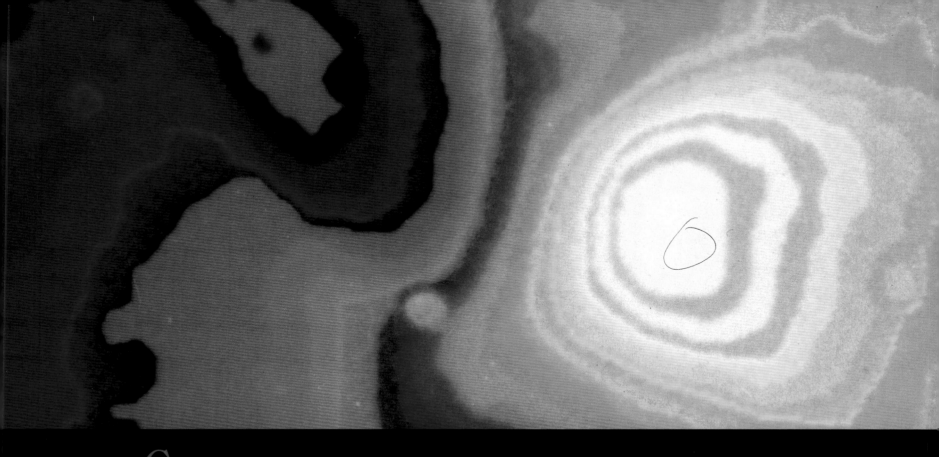

Comets orbit the sun, but they are quite unlike planets. When a comet approaches Earth, it may look spectacular, with a long, glowing tail stretching far across the sky. But comets don't always look like that.

When a comet sweeps in toward the sun, it begins to change. The pressure of sunlight and streams of particles from the sun sweep dust off the comet's surface and evaporate some of the ice. The dust and gas begin to glow and form first a halo, called the coma, and then finally a tail, which may stretch millions of miles.

Around a dozen "new" comets are discovered each year. Most

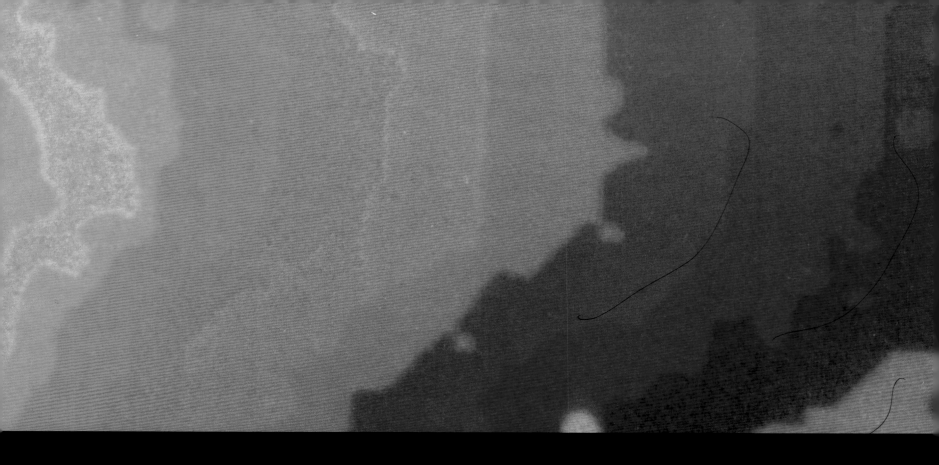

come from the region of icy objects in the Kuiper Belt. Other comets, called long-period comets, arrive from an even more distant region in space called the Oort cloud. These comets can take as long as thirty million years to complete one trip around the sun. Far from the sun, a comet is just a "dirty snowball," a frozen ball of ice a few miles wide, covered by a layer of black dust. This is a photo of Halley's comet on its last visit to Earth in 1986. The small, dark body in the upper left is the comet's nucleus. Halley's comet's next visit to Earth is scheduled in

Meteoroids are small pieces of metal or rock that may have been swept off asteroids or comets. We can't see them in space, but when a meteoroid enters Earth's atmosphere, we see a bright streak of light flashing across the sky. It is then called a meteor. A few of the larger ones may fall to the surface and are called meteorites. Your chances of being hit by a meteorite are small, much less than your chances of being struck by lighting.

Our bodies are made up from some of the same **atoms**
that formed the sun and the stars and created the planets,
moons, asteroids, comets, and meteoroids.

We are all part of the universe.

GLOSSARY

Astronomy—The scientific study of matter in outer space, especially the location, movement, and evolution of the planets, stars, and other objects in space.

Atom—The smallest unit of all matter.

Axis—An imaginary straight line around which a body or geometric object rotates.

Carbon dioxide—A colorless, odorless, and nonflammable gas.

Fahrenheit—A temperature scale where water freezes at 32° and boils at 212°.

Gravity—The natural force of attraction applied by a celestial body, such as Earth, upon objects at or near its surface.

Helium—A colorless, odorless gaseous element occurring in natural gas.

Hydrogen—A colorless, highly flammable gas, the lightest of all gases; it is the most abundant element in the universe.

Methane—An odorless, colorless, and flammable gas.

Milky Way—The galaxy containing our Solar System that can be seen as a band of light stretching across the night sky.

Nuclear—The release of massive amounts of energy at the atomic level.

Nucleus—A core around which other parts of an object or an atom are centered.

Planet—A large, celestial body that moves around, and is lit by, the sun.

Satellite—A celestial body that orbits a planet; for example, Earth's moon.

Solar eclipse—When the moon comes between the sun and Earth and hides some of the light coming from the sun.

Sulfuric acid—A dense and oily liquid formed when water and sulfur dioxide mix with oxygen.

Sunspot—A cooler and darker spot on the sun's surface that appears in groups and is linked to strong magnetic fields.

Telescope—An arrangement of lenses and mirrors that allows people to see very distant objects.

READ MORE ABOUT IT

Smithsonian Institution
www.si.edu

National Aeronautics and Space Administration
www.nasa.gov

Jet Propulsion Laboratory
www.jpl.nasa.gov

The Hubble Space Telescope website
hubblesite.org

PLANETS OF THE SOLAR SYSTEM

	MERCURY	VENUS	EARTH	MARS
Average distance from sun in miles and kilometers	36 million miles/ 58 million km	67 million miles/ 108 million km	93 million miles/ 108 million km	142 million miles/ 228 million km
Revolution in Earth days, Earth years	88 days	224.7 days	365.24 days	687 days
Rotation in Earth days, hours, minutes	58.6 days	243 days	23 hours, 56 mins, 4 sec	24 hours, 37 min, 23 sec
Equatorial diameter in miles	3,032	7,520	7,926.4	4,222
Atmosphere; main gases	Almost none	Carbon dioxide, nitrogen	Nitrogen, oxygen	Carbon dioxide, nitrogen
Surface gravity (Earth = 1)	0.38	0.91	1	0.38
Number of known satellites	0	0	1	2
Rings	0	0	0	0

All information courtesy of NASA's website: http://solarsystem.nasa.gov/planets/index.cfm

SUNSPOTS

JUPITER

MARS

EARTH

VENUS

MERCURY

SUN